D0344490

THE
FRESH PASTA
COOKBOOK

DEVELOPED BY

WILLIAMS
SONOMA

TEST KITCHEN

Photographs Erin Kunkel

weldon**owen**

CONTENTS

Lasagna with Sage Leaves, Butternut
Squash & Brown Butter (page 34)

ABOUT FRESH PASTA

Fresh pasta is a cornerstone of Italian cuisine, and cooks have been crafting it for centuries—mixing, kneading, and rolling out the dough by hand, then cutting and shaping it according to custom and regional preference. The hands-on approach is great for a leisurely weekend, but busy home cooks can take advantage of today's many shortcuts that make fresh pasta an option for weeknight meals, too.

In the Williams Sonoma Test Kitchen, we have made fresh pasta using a variety of methods, each resulting in pasta with a similar texture but different time requirements. Using an electric pasta maker, dough can be mixed, kneaded, and extruded in the form of fresh, ready-to-cook noodles within minutes. With a bit more time in the kitchen, dough can be made in a food processor or in a stand mixer. You can also equip your mixer with attachments for rolling and cutting fresh pasta.

Most recipes in the book start with our basic fresh egg pasta dough. You decide how to make the dough based on your preferred technique, then partner it with the preparations and sauces found in the recipes. Flavor variations to the base recipe—such as spinach, beet, buckwheat, herbs, or squid ink—are easy to incorporate, as are an array of pasta cuts, shapes, and sizes. When the time comes for sauce, this book has you covered with classics like carbonara and basil pesto plus some twists on tradition, such as a mint and pea pesto and spicy chorizo Bolognese. Filled pastas are a favorite too, and you'll find recipes for ravioli and tortellini. Also included are two kinds of gnocchi—classic potato and feather-light ricotta—as well as disk-shaped orecchiette made from semolina flour.

Whether you make fresh pasta by hand or with the help of a machine, you'll be rewarded with incomparable taste and texture.

EQUIPMENT

There are many choices when it comes to making fresh pasta dough. The electric pasta maker offers the quickest route to ready-to-cook fresh pasta, though many prefer to make the dough by hand (or with the help of an electric mixer or food processor). Once the dough is made, pasta may be cut by hand, or with the cutting attachment of either a manual pasta machine or a KitchenAid® stand mixer.

The Philips electric pasta maker mixes and kneads the dough, then extrudes fresh pasta in a variety of cuts—all within minutes.

The hand-cranked pasta machine rolls and cuts fresh pasta by manually feeding the dough through steel rollers, then cutters.

Fresh pasta can be mixed in the KitchenAid® bowl, then fed through a choice of attachments to make cut, shaped, or filled pasta varieties.

MAKING THE DOUGH

Fresh pasta dough can be made using a variety of methods. An electric pasta machine is the quickest option, though the dough can also be made in a stand mixer or food processor, or by hand.

FRESH PASTA DOUGH

2 cups "00" flour, plus more as needed
Pinch of kosher salt
2 large eggs plus 2 large egg yolks
1 tablespoon olive oil
1 tablespoon water

To make the pasta with a Philips Electric Pasta Maker, follow the manufacturer's instructions.

To make the pasta by hand, place the flour on a work surface, mix in the salt, and shape into a mound. Make a well in the center. Add the eggs, egg yolks, oil, and water to the well. Using a fork, beat until blended, keeping the liquid inside the well. Continue to gently beat the egg mixture, gradually drawing in the flour from the sides of the well. When the mixture is too stiff to use the fork, gently mix the dough with your fingertips, gradually drawing in more flour just until a soft, moist, but not sticky ball of dough forms. Using a bench scraper, clean the work surface, discarding any errant bits of dough. Dust the work surface with flour and knead the dough until smooth and elastic, about 10 minutes.

To make the pasta with a KitchenAid®️ stand mixer, in the bowl fitted with the paddle attachment, mix the flour and salt. In a liquid measuring cup, whisk together the eggs, egg yolks, oil, and water. Slowly drizzle the egg mixture into the flour, beating on medium speed until combined, about 1 minute. Turn the dough out onto a lightly floured surface and knead by hand until smooth and firm, about 4 minutes.

To make the pasta in a food processor, in the processor bowl, combine the flour and salt and pulse to mix. In a liquid measuring cup, whisk together the eggs, egg yolks, oil, and water. With the processor running, add the egg mixture in a steady stream and process until combined and the dough forms small clumps that resemble coarse sand; the dough should not form a ball. Stop the machine and pinch the dough; it should come together when pinched but not be sticky. Turn the dough out onto a lightly floured surface and knead by hand until smooth and firm, about 2 minutes.

MAKES ABOUT 1 LB DOUGH

This pasta recipe makes about 1 pound of dough, regardless of the method used to prepare it. The dough should yield enough for about 4 people. Double the recipe for a crowd.

RESTING THE DOUGH

Allow the gluten in the dough to relax before rolling. Place the dough made by any method on a lightly floured work surface, cover with a kitchen towel, and let rest for 15 minutes, or wrap in plastic and refrigerate for up to 2 days; if refrigerated, let the dough stand at room temperature for 30 minutes before using.

ROLLING & CUTTING

To use a manual pasta machine, set the rollers to the widest setting. Divide the dough into 3 equal pieces. Using your hands or a rolling pin, flatten the dough to about ¼ inch so that it will fit through the widest setting. Guide the dough through the rollers. Fold the ends of the pasta sheet over the center like a letter and pass it through the widest setting again, dusting with flour as needed to prevent sticking. Fold and roll the dough again until the dough is silky smooth, 3–4 times.

Switch to the next-thinnest setting and guide the dough through once. Repeat at each setting in sequence, dusting with flour as needed, until the desired thinness is reached. Dust with flour and let rest for 10 minutes before cutting. Attach the cutter accessory and insert the handle into the slot of the chosen cutter, then guide the pasta sheet through the cutter. (See photo at left.) Toss the cut pasta with flour and cover with a kitchen towel until ready to cook.

To use a KitchenAid® pasta roller and cutter, attach the roller attachment to the KitchenAid® and set the rollers to the widest setting. Divide the dough into 3 equal pieces. Using your hands or a rolling pin, flatten the dough to about ¼ inch so that it will fit through the widest setting. With the KitchenAid® on medium-low speed, guide the dough through the rollers. Fold the ends of the pasta sheet over the center like a letter and pass it through the widest setting again, dusting with flour as needed to prevent sticking. Fold and roll the dough again until the dough is silky smooth, 3–4 times.

Switch to the next-thinnest setting and guide the dough through once. Repeat at each setting in sequence until you have reached the desired thinness. Dust with flour as needed to prevent the dough from sticking. Replace the roller attachment with the cutting attachment to cut the pasta into the desired shape. Toss the cut pasta with flour and cover with a kitchen towel until ready to cook.

To roll and cut pasta by hand, divide the dough into 3 equal pieces and roll the pasta on a manual pasta machine as instructed (at left). Generously flour each pasta sheet and fold it in half crosswise, then use a sharp knife or a fluted or flat pasta cutter to cut noodles to the desired width. Toss the cut pasta with flour and cover with a kitchen towel until ready to cook.

buckwheat
pasta

herbed
pasta

beet pasta
(page 58)

spinach pasta
(page 58)

squid ink
pasta

egg pasta
(page 10)

PASTA VARIATIONS

Basic egg pasta can be easily modified with the addition of herbs, vegetable purées, pigmented liquids, and other types of flour—resulting in fresh pasta boasting a range of both flavors and hues. In these pages, look for pastas made from beets, spinach, squid ink, buckwheat, herbs, and semolina flour.

FRESH PASTA WITH SAGE LEAVES

Prepare the Fresh Pasta Dough by any method as directed (page 10), knead, let rest, then roll out the dough into sheets of the desired thinness (page 13). Place 10 sage leaves evenly over half of the dough and fold the dough over, pressing to seal the leaves in place. Return the pasta roller to its widest setting and pass the dough again through each setting until you return to the desired thinness. Cut the pasta by hand into the desired shape.

FRESH SQUID INK PASTA

Prepare the Fresh Pasta Dough by any method as directed (page 10), replacing the water with 2 tablespoons squid ink, and knead until the color is evenly mixed. (If making the dough ahead, refrigerate only up to overnight.) Let the dough rest, then roll out and cut by hand or machine into the desired shape (page 13). Toss the cut pasta with flour and cover with a kitchen towel until ready to cook.

BUCKWHEAT PASTA

Prepare the Fresh Pasta Dough by any method as directed (page 10), replacing the 2 cups "00" flour with 1½ cups buckwheat flour and ½ cup all-purpose flour, and using ½ teaspoon salt. Knead the dough, then let it rest. Roll out the dough and cut by hand or machine into the desired shape (page 13). Toss the cut pasta with flour and cover with a kitchen towel until ready to cook.

HERBED PASTA

Prepare the Fresh Pasta Dough by any method as directed (page 10), adding 2 tablespoons finely chopped fresh sage, rosemary, or thyme leaves to the flour before mixing. Knead the dough, then let it rest. Roll out the dough and cut by hand or machine into the desired shape (page 13). Toss the cut pasta with flour and cover with a kitchen towel until ready to cook.

Angel Hair Pasta with Roasted Cherry Tomatoes & Mascarpone

Angel hair pasta partners beautifully with light and fresh ingredients, and this pairing is no exception. Combining roasted cherry tomatoes and basil with a sauce of melted mascarpone and Parmesan, the dish is bright yet richly flavored.

Make the fresh pasta dough as directed. Roll out the dough and cut into angel hair noodles (page 13) or other pasta shape of your choice.

Preheat the oven to 375°F.

Place the cherry tomatoes and garlic on a baking sheet and spread in a single layer. Drizzle with the oil, season with salt and pepper, and sprinkle with the oregano. Roast until the tomatoes have released their juices and are very tender, about 30 minutes. Transfer the tomatoes and garlic to a large frying pan off the heat.

Meanwhile, bring a large pot of generously salted water to a boil over high heat. Add the pasta and cook until al dente, about 2 minutes. Drain the pasta, reserving ¾ cup of the pasta cooking water.

Set the pan with the tomatoes over medium heat and add the pasta and reserved pasta cooking water. Add the basil, mascarpone, and Parmesan and cook, stirring occasionally, until the sauce is creamy and the pasta is coated with the sauce, about 2 minutes.

Divide the pasta and sauce among 4 bowls. Garnish with basil, a few dollops of mascarpone, and shaved Parmesan and serve.

serves 4

1 lb Fresh Pasta Dough (page 10)

2 pints cherry tomatoes

8 cloves garlic

¼ cup olive oil

Kosher salt and freshly ground pepper

2 tablespoons dried oregano

½ cup loosely packed fresh basil leaves, cut into chiffonade, plus more for serving

¼ cup mascarpone cheese, plus more for serving

½ cup grated Parmesan cheese, plus shaved Parmesan for serving

CHERRY tomatoes hold their shape when cooked, providing both a tasty sauce and enticing bursts of flavor.

Fettuccine with Asparagus, Spring Peas & Creamy Burrata

Fresh spring vegetables shine in this simple preparation, which features fresh fettuccine cloaked in a light sauce of melted burrata cheese, lemon, and butter. Use fresh blanched fava beans or snow peas instead of English peas, if you like.

Make the fresh pasta dough as directed. Roll out the dough and cut into fettuccine noodles (page 13) about ¼ inch wide, or other pasta shape of your choice.

In a large sauté pan over medium heat, warm the oil. Add the shallot and cook, stirring occasionally, until tender, about 2 minutes. Add the asparagus and a pinch each of salt and pepper and cook, stirring occasionally, until bright green and tender, 3–5 minutes. Add the peas, lemon zest and juice, and butter and stir until the butter melts. Stir in the parsley. Remove from the heat and cover to keep warm.

Meanwhile, bring a large pot of generously salted water to a boil over high heat. Add the pasta and cook until al dente, 4–6 minutes. Drain the pasta, reserving 2 cups of the pasta cooking water. Add the pasta to the asparagus mixture. Tear the burrata into pieces, adding it to the pasta and asparagus. Stir until the cheese melts and coats the pasta. Add enough reserved pasta cooking water as needed to loosen the sauce. Adjust the seasoning with salt and pepper.

Divide the pasta and sauce among 4 bowls, garnish with the Parmesan, and serve.

serves 4

1 lb Fresh Pasta Dough (page 10)

2 tablespoons olive oil

1 shallot, finely chopped

1 lb asparagus, trimmed and cut into 2-inch pieces

Kosher salt and freshly ground pepper

¾ cup English peas (fresh or thawed frozen)

Grated zest and juice of 1 lemon

3 tablespoons unsalted butter

¼ cup chopped fresh flat-leaf parsley

½ lb burrata cheese

¼ cup shaved Parmesan cheese

Hand-Cut Noodles with Three-Chile Arrabbiata

Arrabbiata translates to "angry" in Italian, a nod to the assertive spiciness of the chiles. Hand-cut noodles lend subtle texture, although any pasta cut will do.

Preheat the oven to 325°F. Line a baking sheet with parchment paper. Place the tomatoes and smashed garlic cloves on the prepared baking sheet. Toss with 2 tablespoons of the oil, season with salt and black pepper, and spread in a single layer. Roast until the tomatoes shrink and the edges are browned, about 45 minutes. Let cool, then transfer to a food processor and blend until smooth. Set aside.

In a large saucepan over medium heat, warm the remaining 2 tablespoons oil. Add the onion and a pinch each of salt and black pepper. Cook, stirring often, until the onion is tender, about 3 minutes. Add the minced garlic, red pepper flakes, fresh red chile, and Calabrian chile and cook, stirring often, until fragrant, about 1 minute. Stir in the roasted tomato purée and whole peeled tomatoes with their juices. Cook, stirring often and smashing the tomatoes with the back of a wooden spoon, until they break down, about 15 minutes. Adjust the seasoning with salt and black pepper. Remove from the heat and cover to keep warm.

Make the fresh pasta dough as directed. Roll out the dough to the thinnest setting and cut by hand (page 13) into noodles ¼ inch wide.

Meanwhile, bring a large pot of generously salted water to a boil over high heat. Add the pasta and cook until al dente, 4–6 minutes. Drain the pasta, reserving 1 cup of the pasta cooking water. Add the pasta to the sauce and enough reserved pasta cooking water as needed to loosen the sauce.

Divide the pasta and sauce among 4 bowls, garnish with the cheese, and serve.

serves 4

1 lb Roma tomatoes, quartered

4 cloves garlic, smashed, plus 2 cloves garlic, minced

4 tablespoons olive oil

Kosher salt and freshly ground black pepper

1 yellow onion, diced

1 teaspoon red pepper flakes

1 tablespoon minced and seeded fresh red chile, such as thai or jalapeño

1 oil-packed Calabrian chile, drained, seeded, and minced

1 can (15 oz) whole peeled tomatoes

1 lb Fresh Pasta Dough (page 10)

All-purpose flour, for dusting

¼ cup grated Parmesan cheese

Buckwheat Pappardelle with Mushroom Ragoût

Buckwheat pasta has a mild, nutty taste that pairs well with this deeply flavorful mushroom ragoût, enhanced with garlic, sherry, thyme, and olives.

Make the fresh buckwheat pasta dough as directed. Roll out the dough and cut into pappardelle noodles (page 13) about ½ inch wide, or other pasta shape of your choice.

In a large frying pan over medium heat, melt 1 tablespoon of the butter with 1 tablespoon of the oil. Working in 3 batches, add the mushroom, spreading them into a single layer, and cook without stirring until they begin to brown, about 3 minutes. Stir the mushrooms and continue cooking until tender, about 2 minutes longer. Transfer to a plate. Repeat with the remaining mushrooms, adding 1 tablespoon each of the butter and oil to the pan for each batch.

In the same pan over medium-low heat, warm the remaining 1 tablespoon oil. Add the shallots and cook, stirring often, until tender, about 2 minutes. Add the garlic and thyme and cook, stirring occasionally, until fragrant, about 1 minute. Return the mushrooms to the pan and add the sherry, olives, and olive brine. Cook, stirring occasionally, until the liquid is reduced to a glaze, about 2 minutes. Just before serving, reduce the heat to low, stir in the cream, and heat to just below a simmer. Adjust the seasoning with salt and pepper.

Meanwhile, bring a large pot of generously salted water to a boil over high heat. Add the pasta and cook until al dente, 4–6 minutes. Drain the pasta, reserving ¼ cup of the pasta cooking water. Return the pasta to the pot, add the mushroom ragoût and reserved pasta cooking water, and toss to coat the pasta with the sauce.

Divide the pasta and sauce among 4 bowls, garnish with thyme leaves, and serve.

serves 4

1 lb Fresh Buckwheat Pasta Dough (page 15)

3 tablespoons unsalted butter

4 tablespoons olive oil

1½ lb mixed mushrooms, such as cremini, oyster, chanterelle, and shiitake, brushed clean and sliced

2 shallots, finely chopped

3 cloves garlic, minced

2 teaspoons minced fresh thyme, plus thyme leaves for garnish

½ cup dry sherry

½ cup pitted Castelvetrano olives, chopped, plus ¼ cup olive brine

¾ cup heavy cream

Kosher salt and freshly ground pepper

Penne with Fennel Seed Bolognese

Originating in Bologna, Italy, this rustic sauce calls for a long cooking time, allowing the flavors to meld and yielding a dish of luscious complexity.

Make the fresh pasta dough as directed, then cut into penne using a pasta machine or stand mixer attachment. Transfer to a lightly floured baking sheet, toss gently to coat, then spread in a single layer and set aside until ready to use.

In a large saucepan over medium-high heat, warm 3 tablespoons of the oil. Add the ground beef, pork, and veal and cook, breaking it up with a wooden spoon, until cooked through, 8–10 minutes. Add the fennel seeds and cook for 1 minute. Using a slotted spoon, transfer the meat to a plate.

In the same pan over medium-high heat, warm 1 tablespoon oil. Add the carrots, celery, and shallots and cook, stirring occasionally, until the vegetables are tender, about 8 minutes. Add the garlic and cook, stirring, for 1 minute. Reduce the heat to medium and stir in the tomato paste. Add the wine and deglaze the pan, stirring to scrape up any browned bits from the pan bottom. Add the broth and tomatoes and bring to a boil. Add the ground meat, cream, butter, and cheese, and season with salt and pepper. Reduce the heat to low, cover, and cook, stirring occasionally, for 45 minutes.

Preheat the oven to 375°F. Place the shaved fennel on a baking sheet, drizzle with the remaining 2 tablespoons oil, and season with salt and pepper. Roast until tender and slightly crisp, about 25 minutes.

Bring a large pot of generously salted water to a boil over high heat. Add the pasta and cook until al dente, 5–7 minutes. Drain the pasta, add to the sauce, and stir to coat.

Divide the pasta among 4 bowls. Garnish with the roasted fennel, fennel fronds, fennel seeds, and cheese and serve.

serves 4

---

1 lb Fresh Pasta Dough (page 10)

All-purpose flour, for dusting

6 tablespoons olive oil

½ lb ground beef

½ lb ground pork

½ lb ground veal

3 tablespoons fennel seeds, toasted, plus more for garnish

2 carrots, peeled and diced

2 ribs celery, diced

3 shallots, finely chopped

2 cloves garlic, thinly sliced

2½ tablespoons tomato paste

½ cup dry red wine

1 cup chicken broth

1 can (28 oz) crushed tomatoes

¾ cup heavy cream

¼ cup unsalted butter

½ cup grated Parmesan, plus more for serving

Kosher salt and freshly ground pepper

1 small fennel bulb, trimmed and thinly shaved, fronds reserved for garnish

A LAST-MINUTE garnish of roasted shaved fennel adds unexpected texture to this classic dish.

PAIR this fresh spring
dish with crisp white wine,
such as pinot grigio.

Zucchini Ravioli with Mint & Pea Pesto

Shredded zucchini and goat cheese make a wonderfully light filling for these ravioli, complemented by a lemony mint-infused pea pesto.

Make the fresh pasta dough as directed. Divide into 4 pieces and roll out the dough into pasta sheets (page 13); if using a manual pasta machine, roll to the second-thinnest setting. Dust the pasta sheets with flour and cover with a kitchen towel until ready to use.

To make the filling, in a large bowl, stir together the zucchini, garlic, goat cheese, lemon zest, and ricotta. Season with salt and pepper. Set aside.

Make the pesto. Set aside.

To assemble the ravioli, cut the pasta into sheets about 5 inches wide and 10 inches long. Fold each sheet in half lengthwise and press the seam gently to form a crease, then unfold. Spoon a heaping 1 tablespoon of the filling into 4 mounds along one side of each sheet, spacing them about 1½ inches apart . Using a pastry brush, brush the dough edges and around the filling with water. Fold the uncovered half of the dough over the filling and press out any air, then gently press the dough to seal in the filling. Using a pasta cutter, cut out the ravioli. Transfer to a flour-dusted baking sheet. Repeat with the remaining dough and filling.

Bring a large pot of salted water to a gentle boil over medium-high heat. Add the ravioli and cook until al dente, 5–7 minutes.

Meanwhile, transfer the pesto to a large sauté pan and place over medium-low heat. Stir ½ cup of the pasta cooking water into the pesto to loosen it. Using a slotted spoon, transfer the ravioli to the pesto and cook for 1 minute to heat through.

Divide the ravioli and sauce among 4 bowls, garnish with Parmesan and mint leaves, and serve.

serves 4

1 lb Fresh Pasta Dough (page 10)

All-purpose flour, for dusting

FOR THE FILLING

2 zucchini, shredded and drained (about ¾ cup)

1 clove garlic, grated

5 oz goat cheese, at room temperature

2 teaspoons grated lemon zest

1 cup ricotta cheese

Kosher salt and freshly ground pepper

2½ cups Mint & Pea Pesto (page 60)

Grated Parmesan cheese and fresh mint leaves, for garnish

Truffled Fettuccine Alfredo with Artichokes

Artichoke hearts sautéed in truffle oil add woodsy flavor to this updated alfredo. For an elegant finish, shave fresh truffles over the pasta before serving.

Make the fresh pasta dough as directed. Roll out the dough and cut into fettuccine noodles (page 13) about ¼ inch wide, or other pasta shape of your choice.

In a large frying pan over medium-high heat, melt the butter with the truffle oil. Add the artichoke hearts and cook, stirring occasionally, until browned and slightly crisp on the edges, about 10 minutes. Season with salt and pepper. Remove from the heat.

Meanwhile, bring a large pot of generously salted water to a boil over high heat. Add the pasta and cook until al dente, 1½–3 minutes. Drain the pasta, reserving about 3½ cups of the pasta cooking water.

Return the pan with the artichokes to medium heat. Add the pasta, reserved pasta cooking water, and cheese. Cook, stirring until the cheese melts and the sauce thickens and coats the pasta, adding more water or cheese if needed, about 3 minutes. Adjust the seasoning with more truffle oil, salt, and pepper.

Divide the pasta and sauce among 4 bowls, garnish with shaved fresh truffles, if using, and serve.

serves 4

1 lb Fresh Pasta Dough (page 10)

½ cup unsalted butter

3 tablespoons white or black truffle oil, plus more as needed

2 jars (18 oz each) artichoke hearts, drained, rinsed, and quartered

Kosher salt and freshly ground pepper

1 cup packed grated Parmesan cheese, plus more for serving

Fresh truffles, thinly shaved, for serving (optional)

Tagliatelle with Duck Ragoût

Duck is the perfect choice for this hearty sauce. As it simmers, the meat becomes meltingly tender and infused with the flavors of the herbs and spices.

In a large pot or Dutch oven over medium heat, warm the oil. Add the duck legs, skin side down, and cook until golden brown and crisp, 8–10 minutes. Transfer to a platter. Pour off all but 2 tablespoons of the fat from the pot. Return the pot to medium heat, add the onion, carrot, and celery, and cook, stirring often, until very tender and lightly browned, about 5 minutes. Add the garlic, thyme, and oregano and cook, stirring often, for 1 minute. Add the wine and deglaze the pot, stirring to scrape up any browned bits from the bottom, and simmer until reduced by half, about 5 minutes. Stir in the tomato paste, Worcestershire sauce, allspice berries, and broth. Return the duck legs to the pot, making sure they are fully submerged except for the skin. Bring to a simmer, then reduce the heat to medium-low and cook until the duck meat is tender and falling off the bone, about 1½ hours. Transfer the duck to a cutting board and let stand until cool enough to handle. Remove the meat, discarding the skin and bones, and shred the meat into bite-size pieces. Set aside.

While the duck cooks, make the fresh pasta dough as directed. Roll out the dough and cut into tagliatelle noodles (page 13).

Add the flour to the sauce and cook over medium heat, stirring often, until thickened, about 5 minutes. Stir in the cream, season with salt and pepper, and add the duck meat.

Meanwhile, bring a large pot of salted water to a boil over high heat. Add the pasta and cook until al dente, 4–6 minutes. Drain the pasta, reserving 1 cup of the cooking water.

Divide the pasta among 4 bowls. If the sauce is dry, stir in some of the reserved pasta cooking water to loosen it, then ladle the sauce over the pasta. Garnish with oregano and cheese and serve.

serves 4

2 tablespoons olive oil

4 skin-on duck legs (about 2 lbs)

1 red onion, diced

1 carrot, peeled and diced

1 celery stalk, diced

3 cloves garlic, minced

1 tablespoon chopped fresh thyme

1 tablespoon chopped fresh oregano, plus more for garnish

1½ cups dry red wine

3 tablespoons tomato paste

1 tablespoon Worcestershire sauce

1 teaspoon allspice berries

2 cups chicken broth

1 lb Fresh Pasta Dough (page 10)

1 tablespoon all-purpose flour

2 tablespoons heavy cream

Kosher salt and freshly ground pepper

Grated Parmesan cheese, for serving

Bucatini with Pancetta, White Bean Sauce & Garlicky Bread Crumbs

White beans, pancetta, rosemary, and red pepper flakes are an ideal match for these thick, hollow noodles. Bread crumbs add texture and crunch. If bucatini is not an option with your pasta maker, cut thick spaghetti noodles instead.

Make the fresh pasta dough as directed, then cut into bucatini using a pasta machine or stand mixer attachment, or cut into other pasta shape of your choice. Transfer to a lightly floured baking sheet, toss gently to coat, and set aside.

Make the bread crumbs and set aside.

To make the white bean sauce, in a large frying pan over medium-high heat, warm the oil. Add the pancetta and cook, stirring occasionally, until crisp, about 8 minutes. Using a slotted spoon, transfer the pancetta to a paper towel–lined plate. In the same pan, melt the butter. Add the shallots and cook, stirring often, until slightly translucent, about 5 minutes. Add the garlic and cook, stirring often, for 1 minute. Season with salt and black pepper. Add the white beans, broth, rosemary sprigs, and red pepper flakes. Reduce the heat to low, cover, and cook, stirring occasionally, until the beans are slightly broken down and the sauce has thickened, about 20 minutes. Add the pancetta and cook for 3 minutes longer. Remove and discard the rosemary sprigs.

Meanwhile, bring a large pot of salted water to a boil over high heat. Add the pasta and cook until al dente 3–5 minutes. Drain the pasta, reserving ¾ cup of the cooking water. Add the pasta and reserved pasta cooking water to the white bean sauce. Add the cheese and stir to coat the pasta with the sauce.

Divide the pasta and sauce among 4 bowls. Top with the bread crumbs, chopped rosemary, and cheese, and serve.

serves 4

1 lb Fresh Pasta Dough (page 10)

½ cup Garlicky Bread Crumbs (page 61)

FOR THE WHITE BEAN SAUCE

3 tablespoons olive oil

½ lb pancetta, cut into 1-inch pieces

3 tablespoons unsalted butter

2 shallots, finely chopped

4 cloves garlic, thinly sliced

Kosher salt and freshly ground black pepper

2 cans (15 oz each) white beans, drained and rinsed

2 cups chicken broth

2 fresh rosemary sprigs, each about 6 inches long, plus 2 tablespoons chopped fresh rosemary

1½ teaspoons red pepper flakes

½ cup shredded Parmesan cheese, plus more for serving

MAKE the bread
crumbs up to three
hours in advance
and store at room
temperature until
serving time.

Cacio e Pepe Potato Gnocchi with Delicata Squash

The classic Roman preparation *cacio e pepe,* literally "cheese and pepper," features a sauce of coarsely ground pepper, Parmesan, and pecorino. In this version, sweet and earthy delicata squash complements the peppery sauce.

Preheat the oven to 450°F.

Place the potatoes on a wire rack set on a baking sheet. Bake until the potatoes are very tender and easily pierced with a fork, about 50 minutes. Let the potatoes cool slightly, then cut in half lengthwise. Using a spoon, scoop the hot potato flesh into a ricer or a food mill. Press the potato flesh onto a work surface, spreading in an even layer, and let cool for a few minutes. Reduce the oven temperature to 400°F.

Drizzle the egg yolks evenly over the potatoes, making sure the yolks don't pool in any one spot. Sprinkle with the salt, then sift ½ cup of the flour all over the potatoes. Using a pastry blender or a metal bench scraper, cut the flour into the eggs by chopping down repeatedly until the mixture begins to look uniform. Using a bench scraper, gather up the shaggy dough and pat into a loose ball. With the heel of your hand, flatten the ball, then use the bench scraper to fold the dough in half, pressing down again at the end. Sift the remaining ¼ cup flour over the dough and continue to gently press and fold until a uniform dough comes together (make sure to just press down and gently fold, rather than knead, the dough).

Dust a work surface with flour, then dust the dough lightly with flour and shape it into a thick log. Cut off a 2-inch piece of dough and carefully roll into a rope about ½ inch thick. The dough is very delicate and should feel tender, so dust with flour as you go, if needed. Using a bench scraper, cut the rope into 1-inch pieces. If using a gnocchi roller, gently roll each piece of dough on the roller (page 6), then transfer to a well-floured baking sheet. Repeat with the remaining dough.

FOR THE POTATO GNOCCHI

3 lb russet potatoes, scrubbed and pricked with a fork

3 large egg yolks, lightly beaten

1 teaspoon kosher salt

¾ cup all-purpose flour, plus more as needed

Meanwhile, prepare the delicata squash: Place the squash on a baking sheet and spread in a single layer. Top with the thyme sprigs, drizzle with the oil, and season with salt and pepper. Roast until very tender, 20–25 minutes.

In a large frying pan over medium-high heat, melt the butter. Add the pepper and cook until toasted, about 1 minute. Reduce the heat to medium-low, add 1 cup of the Parmesan and ⅓ cup of the pecorino, and whisk until the cheese melts.

Meanwhile, bring a large pot of generously salted water to a boil over high heat. Drop the gnocchi into the boiling water and stir to prevent sticking. Cook until the gnocchi float to the top and are tender without any raw flour taste, 1–2 minutes. Reserve 1¾ cups of the pasta cooking water. Using a spider or a slotted spoon, transfer the gnocchi to the cheese sauce. Add the reserved pasta cooking water, the remaining cheese, and a few grinds of pepper. Cook, stirring occasionally, until the sauce has thickened and coats the gnocchi, about 5 minutes. Taste and adjust the seasoning with salt.

Divide the gnocchi and sauce among 4 bowls. Top each with a few pieces of squash, a thyme sprig, and Parmesan and pecorino cheese and serve.

serves 4

FOR THE DELICATA SQUASH

1 delicata squash, halved lengthwise, seeded, and cut crosswise into ½-inch half-moons

5 fresh thyme sprigs, plus more for garnish

3 tablespoons olive oil

Kosher salt and freshly ground pepper

½ cup unsalted butter

3 teaspoons coarsely ground pepper

1½ cups grated Parmesan cheese, plus more for serving

⅔ cup grated pecorino cheese, plus more for serving

Cacio e Pepe Potato Gnocchi
with Delicata Squash (page 30)

AGE is the star
ttraction in this
pdated classic—
resh leaves are
mbedded in the
asta and fried leaves
re scattered on top.

Lasagna with Sage Leaves, Butternut
Squash & Brown Butter (page 34)

Lasagna with Sage Leaves, Butternut Squash & Brown Butter

This lasagna employs one of the loveliest forms of fresh pasta— delicate, nearly translucent sheets embedded with sage leaves. Layered with roasted butternut squash, béchamel, and fontina, our baked pasta is exceptionally delicious.

Make the fresh pasta dough with sage as directed. Cut the pasta into 6 to 9 sheets, each 8 by 5 inches. Dust the pasta sheets with flour and cover with a kitchen towel until ready to use.

Preheat the oven to 425°F. On a baking sheet, toss together the butternut squash, 2 tablespoons of the oil, the thyme sprigs, 1 teaspoon salt, and ¼ teaspoon black pepper. Spread in a single layer. Roast, stirring once halfway through baking, until the squash is tender and beginning to brown, 30–35 minutes. Transfer the baking sheet to a wire rack. Remove and discard the thyme sprigs. Reduce the oven temperature to 375°F.

In a small saucepan over medium-high heat, melt 4 tablespoons of the butter. Cook, swirling the pan frequently, until the butter is brown and smells nutty, about 5 minutes. Transfer the squash to a large bowl, add the brown butter, and mash coarsely with a fork.

In a medium saucepan over medium-low heat, combine the milk and sage sprigs and heat until the milk begins to bubble at the edges, about 5 minutes. Remove from the heat and let steep for 15 minutes. Discard the sage sprigs.

In another medium saucepan over medium heat, melt the remaining 4 tablespoons butter. When it foams, whisk in the ¼ cup flour and cook, whisking constantly, until it absorbs all of the butter, about 1 minute. Slowly whisk in the sage-infused milk. Bring to a boil over medium heat and cook, stirring constantly, until the béchamel sauce is thickened, about 5 minutes. Season with cayenne, nutmeg, salt, and black pepper.

1 lb Fresh Pasta Dough with Sage (page 15)

All-purpose flour for dusting, plus ¼ cup

3 lb butternut squash, peeled, seeded, and cut into 1-inch cubes

4 tablespoons olive oil

4 fresh thyme sprigs

Kosher salt and freshly ground black pepper

8 tablespoons unsalted butter

3½ cups whole milk

3 fresh sage sprigs, plus 12 whole sage leaves

Pinch of cayenne pepper

Pinch of ground nutmeg

2½ cups grated fontina cheese

¼ cup grated Parmesan cheese

Meanwhile, bring a large pot of generously salted water to a boil over high heat. Working in batches, add the pasta sheets and boil for 30 seconds. Transfer to a baking sheet, arranging them in a single layer.

To assemble the lasagna, spoon ½ cup of the béchamel sauce into a 9 by 13-inch baking dish. Cover with a layer of pasta sheets. Spread half of the butternut squash evenly over the pasta, followed by 1½ cups of the fontina and 1 cup of the béchamel. Repeat with another layer of pasta, the remaining squash, remaining fontina, and 1 cup of the béchamel. Finish with a layer of pasta, the remaining béchamel, and the Parmesan. Cover the dish with aluminum foil and bake for 20 minutes. Uncover the dish and continue baking until the cheese is bubbly and browned, about 15 minutes longer. Remove from the oven and let stand for 10 minutes before serving.

Meanwhile, in a small frying pan over medium-high heat, warm the remaining 2 tablespoons oil until shimmering. Add the sage leaves in a single layer and fry until crisp, about 30 seconds. Transfer to a paper towel–lined plate and sprinkle with salt.

Garnish the lasagna with the fried sage leaves and serve.

serves 6 – 8

Spaghetti & Meatballs with Tomato Sauce

Homemade spaghetti noodles, light-as-a-feather meatballs, and a rich Parmesan-infused tomato sauce make this the ultimate rendition of the pasta favorite. Use top-quality canned tomatoes, such as Italy's San Marzano variety.

Make the fresh pasta dough as directed. Roll out the dough and cut into spaghetti noodles (page 13).

Make the Tomato Ragù; cover and keep warm.

Make the meatballs: In a sauté pan over medium heat, warm 2 tablespoons of the oil. Add the onion and a pinch each of salt and pepper and cook, stirring occasionally, until the onion is caramelized, about 15 minutes. Add the garlic and cook, stirring, for 1 minute. Remove from the heat and let cool.

In a small bowl, whisk together the yogurt and water. Stir in the bread crumbs and let stand for at least 5 minutes. In a large bowl, whisk together the egg, cheese, parsley, basil, and a pinch each of salt and pepper. Stir in the onion and bread crumb mixtures. Add the ground beef and pork and mix gently with your hands until the ingredients are incorporated. Form the mixture into meatballs of about 3 tablespoons each.

In a large frying pan over medium-high heat, warm the remaining 2 tablespoons oil. Working in batches, add the meatballs and cook, turning as needed, until browned on all sides, about 8 minutes per batch. Transfer to the pot with the tomato sauce. After all of the meatballs are in the sauce, bring to a simmer over medium heat and cook, stirring occasionally, until the meatballs are cooked through, about 15 minutes. Discard the cheese rind.

Meanwhile, bring a large pot of salted water to a boil over high heat. Add the pasta and cook until al dente, 4–6 minutes.

Drain the pasta and divide among 4 bowls. Top with the meatballs and sauce, garnish with basil and cheese, and serve.

serves 4

1 lb Fresh Pasta Dough (page 10)

4 cups Tomato Ragù (page 60)

FOR THE MEATBALLS

4 tablespoons olive oil

1 yellow onion, finely diced

Kosher salt and freshly ground pepper

1 clove garlic, minced

¼ cup plain whole milk yogurt

¼ cup water

½ cup dried bread crumbs

1 large egg

½ cup grated Parmesan cheese

½ cup chopped fresh flat-leaf parsley

½ cup chopped fresh basil

¾ lb ground beef

¾ lb ground pork

Fresh basil leaves and grated Parmesan cheese, for serving

USE an ice cream scoop to get the perfect portion of meat, then shape the meatballs gently with your hands.

LINGUINE with pesto is
a classic combination, but
any size of pasta cut works
well in this simple dish.

Spinach Linguine with Basil Pesto

For a modern take, try kale pesto in place of the basil version: replace the basil with 2 cups kale leaves, 1 cup parsley leaves, 1 teaspoon grated lemon zest, and 1 tablespoon lemon juice; swap in toasted walnuts for the pine nuts.

Make the fresh spinach pasta dough as directed. Roll out the dough and cut into linguine noodles (page 13) about ⅛ inch wide, or other pasta shape of your choice. Toss the cut pasta with flour and let dry on the work surface or a drying rack for 15 minutes before cooking.

Turn a food processor on and drop the garlic down the feed tube. Add the basil, pine nuts, and cheese to the processor bowl and pulse until the ingredients are finely chopped, about 10 pulses. Stop the machine and scrape down the sides of the bowl. With the processor running, add the oil in a steady stream and process until smooth, about 30 seconds. Season with salt and pepper.

Meanwhile, bring a large pot of generously salted water to a boil over high heat. Add the pasta and cook until al dente, 2–4 minutes. Drain the pasta, reserving ½ cup of the pasta cooking water, and return the pasta to the pot. Add the pesto and enough reserved pasta cooking water as needed to loosen the sauce.

Divide the pasta and sauce among 4 bowls. Garnish with cheese, pine nuts, and basil leaves and serve.

serves 4

1 lb Fresh Spinach Pasta Dough (page 58)

2 cloves garlic

3 cups fresh basil leaves, plus more for garnish

¼ cup pine nuts, toasted, plus more for garnish

½ cup grated Parmesan cheese, plus more for garnish

½ cup olive oil

Kosher salt and freshly ground pepper

Pappardelle with Chorizo Bolognese

In this updated Bolognese, we riff on tradition by replacing the beef, veal, and pancetta with chorizo, which adds a spicy touch. Broad pappardelle ribbons stand up well to the robust ragù. Be sure to use fresh, not cured, chorizo.

Make the fresh pasta dough as directed. Roll out the dough and cut into pappardelle noodles (page 13) about ½ inch wide, or other pasta shape of your choice.

In a large sauté pan over medium-high heat, warm 1 tablespoon of the oil. Add the chorizo and cook, breaking up the meat with a wooden spoon, until browned, about 5 minutes. Using a slotted spoon, transfer the chorizo to a plate and set aside.

In the same pan over medium heat, warm the remaining 1 tablespoon oil. Add the onion, carrots, and celery and cook, stirring occasionally, until softened, about 5 minutes. Add the garlic, rosemary, and oregano and cook, stirring occasionally, until fragrant, about 1 minute. Add the tomato paste and wine and cook, stirring occasionally, until the liquid is reduced to a glaze, about 2 minutes. Add the diced tomatoes and their juices, the cream, and the reserved chorizo. Reduce the heat to low, and simmer until the sauce thickens, about 20 minutes. Adjust the seasoning with salt and pepper.

Meanwhile, bring a large pot of generously salted water to a boil over high heat. Add the pasta and cook until al dente, about 6 minutes. Drain the pasta, reserving 1 cup of the pasta cooking water. Return the pasta to the pot, add the sauce and enough pasta cooking water as needed to loosen the sauce, and toss to coat.

Divide the pasta and sauce among 4 bowls, garnish with cheese and oregano leaves, and serve.

serves 4

1 lb Fresh Pasta Dough (page 10)

2 tablespoons olive oil

1½ lb fresh pork chorizo, casings removed

1 yellow onion, finely diced

2 carrots, peeled and finely diced

1 celery stalk, finely diced

2 cloves garlic, minced

1 tablespoon minced fresh rosemary

1 teaspoon minced fresh oregano, plus whole leaves, for garnish

1 tablespoon tomato paste

½ cup dry red wine

1 can (14 oz) diced tomatoes

½ cup heavy cream

Kosher salt and freshly ground pepper

Shaved Manchego cheese, for serving

Orecchiette with Broccolini & Italian Sausage

Sturdy, disc-shaped orecchiette stands up well to hearty preparations like this classic pairing of broccolini and lightly browned morsels of Italian sausage. In our twist on tradition, a light celery root purée ties everything together.

Make the fresh orechiette pasta dough, shape, and let dry as directed.

Make the celery root purée. Remove from the heat and cover to keep warm.

In another large sauté pan over medium heat, warm the oil. Add the sausage and cook, breaking up the meat with a wooden spoon, until browned, 6–8 minutes. Using a spider or a slotted spoon, transfer the sausage to a plate. Add the broccolini to the pan and cook, stirring occasionally, until lightly charred and tender, about 5 minutes. Return the sausage to the pan and keep warm.

Meanwhile, bring a large pot of generously salted water to a boil over high heat. Add the pasta and cook until al dente, 8–10 minutes. Drain the pasta, reserving 1 cup of the pasta cooking water. Add the pasta and the celery root purée to the sausage mixture and stir to coat the pasta. Add enough reserved pasta cooking water as needed to loosen the sauce. Adjust the seasoning with salt and pepper.

Divide the pasta and sauce among 4 bowls and serve.

serves 4

1 lb Fresh Orecchiette Pasta (page 59)

3 cups Celery Root Purée (page 60)

1 tablespoon olive oil

1 lb Italian sausage, casings removed, sausage crumbled

2 bunches broccolini, ends trimmed, roughly chopped

Kosher salt and freshly ground pepper

Spaghetti with Saffron-Lemon Clam Sauce

Purchase clams the same day you plan to cook them and make sure they are fresh—they should be tightly closed, a sign they are alive. And the smaller, the better, as those will be the most tender.

Make the fresh pasta dough as directed. Roll out the dough and cut into linguine noodles (page 13) about ⅛ inch wide, or other pasta shape of your choice.

Pour the hot water into a small bowl and crumble in the saffron threads. Let stand for at least 5 minutes.

In a large saucepan over medium heat, melt 2 tablespoons of the butter with the oil. Add the shallots and leek and cook, stirring occasionally, until tender, about 4 minutes. Add the garlic and cook, stirring occasionally, until fragrant, about 1 minute. Add the saffron and water, wine, lemon zest, and 2 tablespoons of the lemon juice. Bring to a boil over medium heat, then reduce the heat to low. Add the clams, discarding any that do not close to the touch, and stir to combine. Cover and steam, shaking the pan occasionally, until the clams have opened, about 4 minutes. Uncover and stir in the mustard and the remaining 4 tablespoons butter and 1 tablespoon lemon juice. Adjust the seasoning with salt and pepper. Discard any unopened clams.

Meanwhile, bring a large pot of generously salted water to a boil over high heat. Add the pasta and cook until al dente, 2–4 minutes. Drain the pasta.

Divide the pasta among 4 bowls. Ladle the clams and broth over the pasta, garnish with parsley and lemon zest, and serve.

serves 4

1 lb Fresh Pasta Dough (page 10)

½ cup hot water

½ teaspoon saffron threads

6 tablespoons unsalted butter

2 tablespoons olive oil

3 shallots, finely chopped

1 leek, white and pale green part, thinly sliced

3 cloves garlic, minced

½ cup dry white wine

2 teaspoons grated lemon zest, plus more for garnish

3 tablespoons fresh lemon juice

2½ lb Manila clams, scrubbed

1 teaspoon Dijon mustard

Kosher salt and freshly ground pepper

Chopped fresh flat-leaf parsley, for garnish

SAFFRON brings subtle aroma and depth of flavor to this classic clam sauce.

Egg Yolk Raviolo with Basil-Parmesan Sauce

Inside each of these generously sized ravioli, a single egg yolk cooks to soft perfection, surrounded by a thick ricotta and Parmesan filling. The runny yolk blends deliciously with the creamy sauce in this richly satisfying dish.

Make the fresh pasta dough as directed. Divide into 4 equal pieces and roll out the dough into pasta sheets; if using a manual pasta machine, roll to the second-thinnest setting (page 13). Dust the pasta sheets with flour and cover with a kitchen towel until ready to use.

To make the filling, in a large bowl, stir together the ricotta, nutmeg, lemon zest, Parmesan, bread crumbs, cream, ½ teaspoon salt, and ½ teaspoon pepper. Taste and adjust the seasoning with more salt and pepper, if needed. Transfer the filling to a piping bag fitted with a ½-inch tip.

To assemble the ravioli, lay out 2 of the sheets and pipe the ricotta filling to form 4 rings per sheet, each about 1 inch wide and ½ inch tall, and spacing them about 1½ inches apart. Place 1 egg yolk in the center of each ricotta ring. Using a pastry brush, brush the dough with water around the edges and in between the ricotta rings. Place the remaining pasta sheets over the top of the sheets with the filling and gently press to remove the excess air. Using a sharp knife, cut the raviolo apart between the ricotta rings. Using a fork, seal the edges of each raviolo. Cover with the kitchen towel while you make the sauce.

1 lb Fresh Pasta Dough (page 10)

FOR THE FILLING

1 container (15 oz) ricotta cheese

¼ teaspoon ground nutmeg

Grated zest of 1 lemon

¼ cup grated Parmesan cheese

3 tablespoons dried bread crumbs

3 tablespoons heavy cream

Kosher salt and freshly ground pepper

8 large egg yolks

To make the sauce, in a large sauté pan over medium-low heat, melt the butter. Add the garlic and cook, stirring occasionally, until fragrant, about 1 minute. Add the cream, basil, and Parmesan and stir until combined. Cook, stirring frequently, until the sauce thickens slightly, 3- 5 minutes. Adjust the seasoning with salt and pepper. Keep warm.

Meanwhile, bring a large pot of generously salted water to a gentle boil over medium-high heat. Add the ravioli and cook until al dente, 5–7 minutes. Reserve 1 cup of the pasta cooking water. Add enough of the reserved pasta water to the sauce as needed to loosen it.

Using a spider or a slotted spoon, carefully transfer 2 ravioli to each of 4 shallow bowls, then gently spoon the sauce over the tops. Garnish with shaved Parmesan and basil, and serve.

serves 4

FOR THE CREAMY BASIL-PARMESAN SAUCE

2 tablespoons unsalted butter

3 cloves garlic, minced

1 cup heavy cream

1 cup fresh basil leaves, finely chopped

¼ cup grated Parmesan cheese

Kosher salt and freshly ground pepper

Shaved Parmesan cheese and fresh basil, for garnish

FRESH beet pasta is bright red when raw but turns a delightful rose-colored hue when cooked.

Hand-Cut Beet Pasta with Hazelnut-Sage Butter & Goat Cheese

Rosy ribbons of beet pasta form a colorful backdrop for hazelnut-infused brown butter garnished with crisp sage leaves. A fluted pastry wheel gives the pappardelle a decorative edge, but a straight cut would work equally well.

Make the fresh beet pasta dough as directed. Roll out the dough into pasta sheets (page 13). Lay out 1 sheet of pasta on a floured work surface and cut in half crosswise. Using a fluted or a flat pasta cutter, cut each piece into noodles about 1 inch thick. Toss the cut pasta with flour and let dry on the work surface or a drying rack for 15 minutes before cooking.

In a large sauté pan over medium heat, melt the butter. Add the sage leaves and cook until the butter is lightly browned and the sage leaves are crisp, about 4 minutes. Using a spider or a slotted spoon, transfer the sage leaves to a paper towel-lined plate. Raise the heat to medium-high, add the hazelnuts to the pan, and cook, stirring occasionally, until the nuts are lightly browned, about 3 minutes. Season with salt and pepper. Remove the pan from the heat.

Meanwhile, bring a large pot of generously salted water to a boil over high heat. Add the pasta and cook, stirring with a wooden spoon to prevent sticking and tasting at regular intervals, until al dente, about 2 minutes. Drain the pasta, reserving ½ cup of the pasta cooking water

Set the pan with the hazelnut-butter sauce over medium heat. Transfer the pasta to the pan, add the pasta cooking water, and toss to coat the pasta with the sauce.

Divide the pasta and sauce among 4 bowls, top with clusters of goat cheese and the fried sage leaves, and serve.

serves 4

1 lb Fresh Beet Pasta Dough (page 58)

All-purpose flour, for dusting

1 cup unsalted butter

15 fresh sage leaves

½ cup hazelnuts, chopped

Kosher salt and freshly ground pepper

½ lb goat cheese

Orecchiette with Crispy Pancetta, Peas & Melted Leeks

Known to Italians as "little ears," orecchiette originated in the Puglia region. The disk-shaped pasta includes some semolina flour, which gives it a slightly coarser texture and pleasantly dense and chewy bite when cooked.

Make the fresh orechiette pasta dough, shape, and let dry as directed.

In a large frying pan over medium-high heat, warm the oil. Add the pancetta and cook, stirring occasionally, until crisp, about 5 minutes. Using a slotted spoon, transfer the pancetta to a plate and set aside.

Reduce the heat to low and melt 4 tablespoons of the butter in the pan. Add the leeks and cook, stirring occasionally, until they begin to soften, about 5 minutes. Add the garlic, season with salt and pepper, and cook, stirring occasionally, until extremely tender and falling apart, 10–15 minutes longer. Add the reserved pancetta, the peas, and wine and cook, stirring occasionally, until the peas are just tender, about 1 minute.

Meanwhile, bring a large pot of generously salted water to a boil over high heat. Add the pasta and cook until al dente, 6–8 minutes. Drain the pasta, reserving 1 cup of the pasta cooking water. Transfer the orecchiette to the sauce. Raise the heat to medium and bring to a gentle simmer. Add the cheese and reserved pasta cooking water and cook, stirring occasionally, until the cheese melts and the pasta is coated with the sauce, about 3 minutes. Adjust the seasoning with salt and pepper.

Divide the pasta and sauce among 4 bowls, top with the pea shoots and cheese, and serve.

serves 4

1 lb Fresh Orrechiette Pasta (page 59)

3 tablespoons olive oil

1 lb pancetta, cut into bite-size pieces

½ cup unsalted butter

5 leeks, halved lengthwise and thinly sliced crosswise (white and pale green part)

2 cloves garlic, grated

Kosher salt and freshly ground pepper

1½ cups frozen peas, slightly thawed

¼ cup dry white wine

1 cup grated Parmesan cheese, plus more for serving

2 cups pea shoots

FRESH pea shoots add
bright flavor and crisp
texture to this spring dish.

Penne alla Norma with Smoked Mozzarella & Hazelnut Gremolata

In this contemporary adaptation of penne alla Norma, the traditional trio of eggplant, tomatoes, and basil gets a boost from smoked mozzarella cheese and a lemony herb and hazelnut gremolata.

Make the fresh pasta dough as directed, then cut into penne using a pasta machine or stand mixer attachment. Transfer to a lightly floured baking sheet, toss gently to coat, then spread in a single layer and set aside until ready to use.

In a large nonstick frying pan over medium heat, warm ¼ cup of the oil until shimmering. Add half of the eggplants and 1 teaspoon of the oregano and season with salt. Cook, stirring frequently, until the eggplants are browned on all sides, about 10 minutes. Transfer to a plate. Repeat with another ¼ cup of the oil and the remaining eggplants and oregano.

In a large saucepan over medium heat, warm the remaining 1 tablespoon oil. Add the garlic and red pepper flakes and cook, stirring occasionally, until fragrant, about 1 minute. Add the tomatoes and basil sprig, reduce the heat to low, and simmer until the flavors blend, about 10 minutes. Adjust the seasoning with salt and black pepper.

Meanwhile, make the gremolata. Set aside.

Bring a large pot of generously salted water to a boil over high heat. Add the pasta and cook until al dente, 5–7 minutes. While the pasta is cooking, add the eggplants to the tomato sauce and heat, stirring occasionally, until warmed through.

Drain the pasta, reserving ½ cup of the pasta cooking water. Add the pasta, reserved pasta cooking water, and cheese to the sauce. Stir gently until mixed and the cheese is melted.

Divide the pasta and sauce among 4 bowls, top with the hazelnut gremolata, and serve.

serves 4

1 lb Fresh Pasta Dough (page 10)

½ cup plus 1 tablespoon olive oil

2 large eggplants (about 2 lb total weight), cut into 1-inch cubes

2 teaspoons dried oregano

Kosher salt and freshly ground black pepper

4 cloves garlic, minced

½ teaspoon red pepper flakes

1 can (28 oz) crushed tomatoes

1 sprig fresh basil

½ cup Hazelnut Gremolata (page 60)

1 cup grated smoked mozzarella cheese

Ricotta Gnocchi with Sweet Corn, Pecorino & Chives

Thanks to the addition of ricotta cheese, these gnocchi are exceptionally light and tender. This version of the bite-size dumplings are cooked using a short-cut technique: the dough is piped from a pastry bag directly into boiling water.

To make the gnocchi, in a food processor, combine the ricotta, egg yolks, Parmesan, and 2 teaspoons salt and process until smooth. Add the flour and process until just incorporated. Transfer the ricotta mixture to a piping bag fitted with a 1-inch tip. Refrigerate until ready to use, or for up to 8 hours.

To make the corn sauce, in a large sauté pan over medium heat, melt the butter. Add the onion, coriander, and a pinch each of salt and black pepper. Cook, stirring occasionally, until the onion is tender, about 3 minutes. Add the garlic and cook, stirring occasionally, until fragrant, about 1 minute. Add the corn and cook, stirring occasionally, until just tender, about 2 minutes. Add the wine and simmer until reduced by half, about 3 minutes. Taste and adjust the seasoning with salt and black pepper.

Meanwhile, bring a large pot of generously salted water to a boil over high heat. Pipe the gnocchi over the water, using a small, sharp knife to cut at the tip into 1-inch pieces. Cook until the gnocchi float to the top, 2–4 minutes. Reserve 1 cup of the pasta cooking water. Using a spider or a slotted spoon, carefully transfer the gnocchi to the corn sauce and stir to coat, adding enough reserved pasta cooking water as needed to loosen the sauce.

Divide the gnocchi and sauce among 4 bowls. Sprinkle with the cheese, chives, and red pepper flakes and serve.

serves 4

FOR THE RICOTTA GNOCCHI

1 container (15 oz) ricotta cheese

3 large egg yolks

1 cup grated Parmesan cheese

Kosher salt

1 cup all-purpose flour

FOR THE CORN SAUCE

6 tablespoons unsalted butter

1 yellow onion, diced

1 teaspoon ground coriander

Kosher salt and freshly ground black pepper

2 cloves garlic, minced

Kernels from 2 ears of corn (about 1½ cups)

½ cup dry white wine

¼ cup grated pecorino cheese

2 tablespoons chopped fresh chives

Red pepper flakes, for garnish

HOLLOW strands of bucatini are an excellent partner to this creamy sauce.

Bucatini Carbonara with Brussels Sprouts

The last-minute addition of eggs contributes rich flavor and a velvety sheen to this classic sauce. Here, pan-roasted brussels sprouts lend a fresh finish.

Make the fresh pasta dough as directed, then cut into bucatini noodles using a pasta machine or stand mixer attachment. Gently toss the noodles with flour and set aside.

In a large frying pan over medium-high heat, warm 2 tablespoons of the oil. Add the pancetta and cook, stirring occasionally, until crisp, about 8 minutes. Using a slotted spoon, transfer the pancetta to a paper towel–lined plate and set aside. Add ¼ cup of the butter to the pan, then add the brussels sprouts and cook, stirring often, until lightly browned and tender, about 10 minutes. Using the slotted spoon, transfer the brussels sprouts to another plate and set aside.

In the same pan over medium heat, warm the remaining 1 tablespoon oil. Add the shallots and cook, stirring often, until softened, about 3 minutes. Add the garlic and cook, stirring occasionally, until the shallots are caramelized, about 3 minutes. Add the cream and remaining ¼ cup butter, reduce the heat to low, and cook, stirring often, until thickened, about 5 minutes. Stir in the cheese. Season with salt and pepper. Remove from the heat and cover to keep warm.

Meanwhile, bring a large pot of salted water to a boil over high heat. Add the pasta and cook until al dente, 1–2 minutes. Drain the pasta, reserving ½ cup of the pasta cooking water.

Transfer the pasta to the warm cream sauce and add the egg yolks. Working quickly, use tongs to mix the yolks with the pasta and sauce until the pasta is evenly coated, about 2 minutes. Add enough of the reserved pasta cooking water as needed to loosen the sauce, stir to mix, then add the pancetta. Adjust the seasoning with salt and pepper. Divide the pasta and sauce among 4 bowls, top with the brussels sprouts and shaved cheese, and serve.

serves 4

1 lb Fresh Pasta Dough (page 10)

All-purpose flour, for dusting

3 tablespoons olive oil

10 oz pancetta, cut into 1-inch pieces

½ cup unsalted butter

¾ lb brussels sprouts, trimmed and thinly sliced

2 shallots, finely chopped

2 cloves garlic, minced

2 cups heavy cream

¼ cup grated Parmesan cheese, plus shaved cheese, for serving

Kosher salt and freshly ground pepper

7 large egg yolks, lightly beaten

Squid Ink Tagliatelle with Crab & Calabrian Chiles

Aromatic squid ink lends a silky black hue and subtle taste of the sea to traditional egg pasta. Here, chile-spiced crab and garlicky bread crumbs complement this classic pasta variety of the Italian coast.

Make the squid ink pasta dough as directed. Roll out the dough to the thinnest setting and cut into tagliatelle noodles (page 13).

Make the bread crumbs. Set aside.

In a large sauté pan over medium heat, melt the butter. Add the shallot, celery, and a pinch each of salt and pepper and cook, stirring occasionally, until the shallot and celery are tender, about 3 minutes. Add the Calabrian chiles, lemon zest, and crabmeat and cook, stirring occasionally, until just warmed through, 2–4 minutes. Season to taste with salt and pepper. Remove from the heat and cover to keep warm.

Meanwhile, bring a large pot of generously salted water to a boil over high heat. Add the pasta and cook until al dente, 4–6 minutes. Drain the pasta, reserving 1 cup of the pasta cooking water. Add the pasta to the crabmeat mixture and stir gently to coat the pasta. Add enough reserved pasta cooking water as needed to loosen the sauce.

Divide the pasta and sauce among 4 bowls, garnish with dollops of the crème fraîche, and serve.

serves 4

1 lb Squid Ink Pasta (page 15)

½ cup Garlicky Bread Crumbs (page 61)

5 tablespoons unsalted butter

1 shallot, finely chopped

2 celery stalks, thinly sliced

Kosher salt and freshly ground pepper

2 tablespoons oil-packed Calabrian chiles, mashed

Grated zest of 1 lemon

½ lb cooked crabmeat, picked over for shell fragments

¼ cup crème fraîche

A FAVORITE in Italy's Veneto region, squid ink pasta has an exotic appearance and slight brininess.

Five-Spice Pork Tortellini with Parmesan Cream Sauce

Mastering the technique for filling and folding these little dumplings may take some practice, but the result is worth the effort. Five-spice powder adds a unique twist to this otherwise classic Italian dish.

To make the filling, in a large frying pan over medium heat, warm the oil. Add the shallot and cook, stirring occasionally, until tender, about 2 minutes. Add the ground pork, prosciutto, and five-spice powder and cook, breaking up the meat with a wooden spoon, until the ground pork is browned and cooked through, 4–6 minutes. Add the wine and cook, stirring occasionally, until reduced by half, about 3 minutes. Let cool to room temperature. Transfer the pork mixture to a food processor and process to an even consistency. Add the Parmesan and egg and process until blended. Transfer the filling to a piping bag fitted with a ¼-inch tip and set aside.

Make the pasta as directed. Divide the dough into 4 equal pieces and roll out into pasta sheets (page 13); If using a manual pasta machine, roll to the second thinnest setting. Arrange the pasta sheets in a single layer on lightly floured baking sheets, dust with more flour, and cover with a kitchen towel until ready to use.

To assemble the tortellini, working in batches and keeping the the pasta covered when not using, cut the pasta sheets into 2½-inch squares. Pipe 1 teaspoon of the filling into the center of each square. Fold each square diagonally into a triangle, pressing the edges together to remove the excess air. Bring the bottom 2 corners of the triangle together to form a circle and press to tightly seal. Place on a floured baking sheet and cover with a kitchen towel while making the rest of the tortellini. For longer storage, cover with plastic wrap and refrigerate for up to 1 day.

FOR THE FILLING

1 tablespoon olive oil

1 shallot, finely chopped

6 oz ground pork

6 oz prosciutto, roughly chopped

1 tablespoon Chinese five-spice powder

¼ cup dry white wine

1½ cups grated Parmesan cheese

1 large egg

1 lb Fresh Pasta Dough (page 10)

All-purpose flour, for dusting

To make the sauce, in a large sauté pan over medium heat, melt the butter. Add the garlic and cook, stirring occasionally, until fragrant, about 1 minute. Stir in the flour and cook until it absorbs all of the butter, about 1 minute. Stir in the broth a few tablespoons at a time, making sure it is completely absorbed before adding more. Add the cream, Parmesan, and mascarpone and stir to combine. Adjust the seasoning with salt and pepper. Remove from the heat; cover to keep warm.

Meanwhile, bring a large pot of generously salted water to a boil over high heat. Add the tortellini and cook until al dente, 3–5 minutes. Using a slotted spoon, transfer the tortellini to the sauce, reserving 1 cup of the pasta cooking water. Gently stir the tortellini to coat them with the sauce, adding enough reserved pasta cooking water as needed to loosen the sauce.

Divide the tortellini and sauce among 4 bowls, garnish with chives, and serve.

serves 4

FOR THE PARMESAN CREAM SAUCE

¼ cup unsalted butter

4 cloves garlic, minced

2 tablespoons all-purpose flour

1 cup chicken broth

½ cup heavy cream

½ cup grated Parmesan cheese

¼ cup mascarpone cheese

Kosher salt and freshly ground pepper

Chopped fresh chives, for garnish

BASIC RECIPES

Spinach Pasta

10 oz baby spinach leaves
2 large eggs
2½ cups all-purpose flour,
plus more for dusting
1 teaspoon kosher salt

MAKES ABOUT 1 LB DOUGH

Rinse the spinach and drain briefly. Place the damp spinach in a large frying pan, set over medium heat, and cook, tossing occasionally, until the spinach wilts, 2–3 minutes. Transfer to a fine-mesh sieve and drain well. When cool, wrap the spinach in a kitchen towel and squeeze thoroughly dry.

Transfer the spinach to a food processor, add the eggs, and process to a smooth purée, stopping to scrape down the sides of the bowl as needed. Add the flour and salt and process until the dough forms small clumps; it should come together when pinched. Transfer the dough to a lightly floured work surface and knead until it is even in color and not sticky, about 3 minutes, adding more flour as needed. Place the dough on a lightly floured work surface, cover with an overturned bowl, and let rest at room temperature for 15 minutes, or wrap in plastic and refrigerate for up to 2 days; if refrigerated, let the dough stand at room temperature for 30 minutes before using.

Roll out and cut the pasta by hand or machine into the desired shape (page 13).

Beet Pasta

2 small red beets (about 7 oz total
weight), trimmed and rinsed
2 tablespoons olive oil
2 tablespoons water
2⅓ cups all-purpose flour,
plus more as needed
1½ teaspoons kosher salt
1 large egg plus 5 large egg yolks

MAKES ABOUT 1 LB DOUGH

Bring a large pot of water to a boil over high heat. Add the beets and cook until they are fork-tender, about 45 minutes. Drain the beets and let cool completely, then peel and cut into quarters. In a food processor, combine the beets, oil, and water and process until smooth and creamy. (Alternatively, use a small hand blender.) Set the beet purée aside.

Place the flour on a work surface, mix in the salt, and shape the flour into a mound. Using your fingertips, make a well in the center, making sure the sides are high enough to hold the eggs. Add the egg, egg yolks, and 4 tablespoons of the beet purée to the well. Using a fork, beat until the eggs and beet purée are blended and a cohesive mixture forms. Slowly begin to incorporate the flour until a wet, sticky dough forms. Using a bench scraper, continue to fold in the flour until the dough comes together. The dough will feel dry and somewhat rough on the exterior.

Using the heel of your hand, knead the dough until it becomes a cohesive color and develops a smooth, elastic texture, about 5 minutes. If the dough feels too wet, add more flour in 1-teaspoon increments. If the dough feels too dry, dampen your hands slightly and continue to knead for 1 minute. Place the dough on a lightly floured work surface, cover with an overturned bowl, and let rest at room temperature for 15 minutes, or wrap in plastic and refrigerate for up to 2 days; if refrigerated, let the dough stand at room temperature for 30 minutes before using.

Roll out and cut the pasta by hand or machine into the desired shape (page 13). The dough will be very delicate and often sticky, so dust with flour as needed.

Orecchielle Pasta

1¼ cups semolina flour, plus more
as needed
1¼ cups all-purpose flour
Pinch of kosher salt
⅔ cup water, plus more as needed

MAKES ABOUT 1 LB DOUGH

Place the semolina flour and all-purpose flour on a work surface, mix in the salt, and shape the flour into a mound. Using your fingertips, make a well in the center, making sure the sides are high enough to hold the water. Add the water to the well. Using a fork, gradually draw the flour from the sides of the well into the water and beat gently, always in the same direction, to combine the flour with the liquid.

Secure the flour wall with your other hand until the liquid has absorbed enough flour that it will not flow over the wall.

When the mixture is too stiff to use the fork, begin using both hands, gradually drawing in the flour from the bottom of the wall, until a soft, moist, but not sticky ball of dough forms. If the dough will not absorb more flour without becoming stiff, do not use all of it. If it is too soft, add more flour, a spoonful at a time. Clean the work surface, dust it lightly with flour, and flatten the ball of dough into a disk.

Using the heel of your hand, push the dough down and away from you, fold it in half back toward you, rotate a quarter turn, and repeat the kneading process until the dough is smooth and elastic, about 10 minutes.

Place the dough on a lightly floured work surface, cover with an overturned bowl, and let rest at room temperature for 15 minutes, or wrap in plastic and refrigerate for up to 2 days; if refrigerated, let the dough stand at room temperature for 30 minutes before using.

Shape the dough into a ball and cut into 4 equal pieces. Working with 1 piece of dough at a time, and keeping the rest covered with a damp paper towel, roll the dough into a log. Cut into pieces slightly larger than a pea. Roll each piece of dough into a small ball, then press your thumb in the center to create a thin, curved disk shape. Transfer to a baking sheet dusted with semolina flour. Repeat with the remaining dough. Let the orecchiette dry uncovered at room temperature for 1–2 hours.

Tomato Ragù

2 tablespoons olive oil

1 yellow onion, thinly sliced

Kosher salt and freshly ground pepper

4 cloves garlic, minced

1 tablespoon capers, roughly chopped

2 tablespoons sherry vinegar

2 cans (28 oz each) whole peeled tomatoes with juices

1 Parmesan cheese rind (about 4 inches long)

MAKES ABOUT 4 CUPS

In a large pot over medium heat, warm the oil. Add the onion and a big pinch each of salt and pepper and cook, stirring occasionally, until the onion is tender, about 3 minutes. Add the garlic, capers, and vinegar and cook, stirring occasionally, until fragrant, about 1 minute. Add the tomatoes and their juices and the cheese rind and bring to a simmer, then cook, stirring occasionally, until the tomatoes break down and the sauce thickens, about 20 minutes. Adjust the seasoning with salt and pepper. Discard the cheese rind just before serving.

Mint & Pea Pesto

2 ½ cups fresh peas, blanched and drained

2 cups fresh mint leaves

1 cup fresh basil leaves

½ cup grated Parmesan cheese

3 tablespoons fresh lemon juice

3 cloves garlic

¾ cup olive oil, plus more as needed

Kosher salt and freshly ground pepper

MAKES ABOUT 2½ CUPS

In a food processor, combine the peas, mint, basil, Parmesan, lemon juice, and garlic and pulse until a cohesive paste forms. Stop the machine and scrape down the sides of the bowl. With the processor running, add the oil in a steady stream and process until the mixture has emulsified slightly and lightened in color. Season with salt and pepper.

Garlicky Bread Crumbs

6 oz coarse country bread, crusts removed, torn into pieces

¼ cup olive oil

4 cloves garlic, grated

1 teaspoon grated lemon zest

Kosher salt and freshly ground black pepper

MAKES ABOUT ½ CUP

In a food processor, process the bread until fine crumbs form. In a sauté pan over medium-low heat, warm the oil. Add the bread crumbs, garlic, and lemon zest and cook, stirring frequently, until the bread crumbs are golden brown and crisp, 6–8 minutes. Season with salt and pepper.

Celery Root Purée

¼ cup unsalted butter

1 yellow onion, diced

1 clove garlic, minced

1 celery root, peeled and thinly sliced

1 cup heavy cream

Kosher salt and freshly ground pepper

¾ cup chicken broth

3 tablespoons crème fraîche

MAKES ABOUT 3 CUPS

In a large sauté pan over medium heat, melt the butter. Add the onion and cook, stirring occasionally, until tender, about 3 minutes. Add the garlic and cook, stirring often, until fragrant, about 1 minute. Add the celery root, cream, and a big pinch each of salt and pepper. Cook, stirring occasionally, until the celery root is very tender, about 15 minutes. Let cool slightly, then transfer the celery root mixture to a blender and blend on high speed until smooth, about 1 minute. Return the purée to the pan and stir in the broth and crème fraîche. Adjust the seasoning with salt and pepper. Keep warm.

Hazelnut Gremolata

⅓ cup chopped fresh flat-leaf parsley

2 tablespoons chopped fresh basil

2 tablespoons chopped, toasted, and skinned hazelnuts

½ teaspoon grated lemon zest

1 clove garlic, minced

1 tablespoon olive oil

1 teaspoon fresh lemon juice

Kosher salt and freshly ground black pepper

MAKES ABOUT ½ CUP

In a bowl, stir together the parsley, basil, hazelnuts, lemon zest, and garlic. Add the oil and lemon juice and stir to combine. Season with salt and pepper.

GLOSSARY

Bench Scraper A bench scraper, also known as a pastry scraper or dough scraper, is used in working with pastry, bread, and other dough. It is a flat, rectangular piece of metal or plastic, often with a low handle on the top. It is used to portion bread dough cleanly, provide support for lifting and turning dough, and to scrape excess flour and dough from a work surface.

Gnocchi Roller A small wood board with ridges for shaping traditional gnocchi. The board is held at an angle to the work surface by a long handle. Small rounds of dough are rolled over the board to form ridged rounds of gnocchi.

Spider A type of skimmer comprised of a long handle attached to a wide, shallow wire-mesh basket. Often used in Asian cooking, spiders are also useful for lifting pasta from boiling water.

"00" Flour Italians use "00" flour *(doppio zero)* in their fresh pastas, and the flour is now widely available in the United States as well. It is a soft-wheat flour that is almost powdery and yields a particularly light and porous dough. If you cannot find it, unbleached all-purpose flour is the best substitute.

INDEX

The Fresh Pasta Cookbook

Conceived and produced by Weldon Owen, Inc.
in collaboration with Williams Sonoma, Inc.
3250 Van Ness Avenue, San Francisco, CA 94109

A WELDON OWEN PRODUCTION
1045 Sansome Street, Suite 100
San Francisco, CA 94111
www.weldonowen.com

WELDON OWEN, INC.
President & Publisher Roger Shaw
SVP, Sales & Marketing Amy Kaneko
Finance & Operations Director Thomas Morgan

Associate Publisher Amy Marr
Senior Editor Lisa Atwood

Creative Director Kelly Booth
Art Director Marisa Kwek
Production Designer Howie Severson

Production Director Michelle Duggan
Production Manager Sam Bissell
Imaging Manager Don Hill

Photographer Erin Kunkel
Food Stylist Emily Caneer
Prop Stylist Kelly Allen

Printed in the USA
First printed in 2018
10 9 8 7 6 5 4 3 2 1

Library of Congress Cataloging-in-Publication
data is available.

ISBN: 978-1-68188-400-4

Weldon Owen is a division of Bonnier Publishing USA

ACKNOWLEDGMENTS

Weldon Owen wishes to thank the following people for their
generous support in producing this book: Amy Allgood, Kris Balloun, Lesley Bruynesteyn,
Olivia Caminiti, Josephine Hsu, Eve Lynch, Kayla Minko, Elizabeth Parson, and Karen Zuniga.

Additional photo credits: Stocksy (page 11), Shutterstock (page 12)